FANTANSTIC
DOT-TO-DOT
PUZZLES

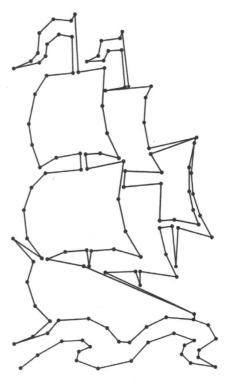

Conceptis Puzzles

PUZZLE
WRIGHT
PRESS

New York

**PUZZLE
WRIGHT
PRESS**

New York

An Imprint of Sterling Publishing
387 Park Avenue South
New York, NY 10016

ISBN 978-1-4549-1197-5

Distributed in Canada by Sterling Publishing
c/o Canadian Manda Group, 165 Dufferin Street
Toronto, Ontario, Canada M6K 3H6
Distributed in the United Kingdom by GMC Distribution Services
Castle Place, 166 High Street, Lewes, East Sussex, England BN7 1XU
Distributed in Australia by Capricorn Link (Australia) Pty. Ltd.
P.O. Box 704, Windsor, NSW 2756, Australia

For information about custom editions, special sales, and premium and corporate purchases,
please contact Sterling Special Sales at 800-805-5489 or specialsales@sterlingpublishing.com.

Manufactured in China

6 8 10 9 7 5

www.puzzlewright.com

•••••••••••••••••• **Contents** ••••••••••••••••••

Do you like to connect dots and make fantastic line art? If so, you've come to the right place! The 80 puzzles that follow will have you connecting thousands of dots and marveling at your own artistic skill. All you need is a pencil, a keen eye, a steady hand, and the ability to count into the hundreds. All set? Then let's get started!

If you've never solved a dot-to-dot puzzle before, here's how it works: find the number 1 somewhere on the page, then place your pencil on the dot next to it. Draw a straight line over to the dot next to the number 2, then draw another line to the dot next to the number 3, and so on. Eventually, you'll run out of dots and the picture will be complete (the final dot will always be a star). Feel free to hold it at arm's length and admire your handiwork!

You'll notice that sometimes dots have been placed so they're overlapping, but that's okay; the dot with the lowest number will always be on top, and you'll see any future dots in that location peeking out from beneath the first dot. You may need to visually survey an area to determine which dot goes with which number, and remember that sometimes the next dot may be back the way you came from (or even along the same path you just created).

After you've completed each puzzle in pencil, you might want to go back over the correct path with a pen or colored pencil. You could even bust out the crayons and do some coloring! In any case, please enjoy the puzzles that follow and check out the other books in the Connectivity series. Visit us at www.conceptispuzzles.com for more ways to have fun and get smart.

—Conceptis Puzzles

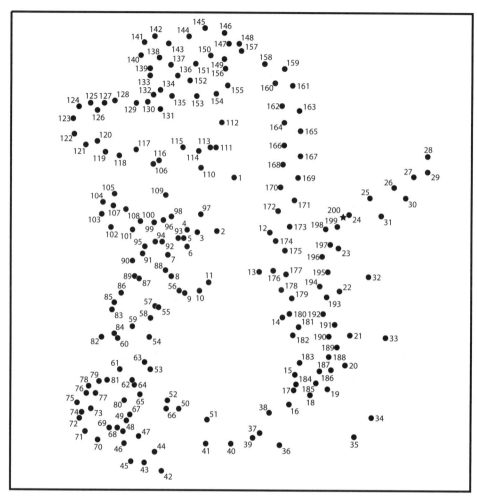

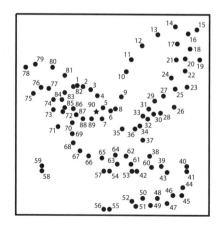

ANSWERS, PAGE 78

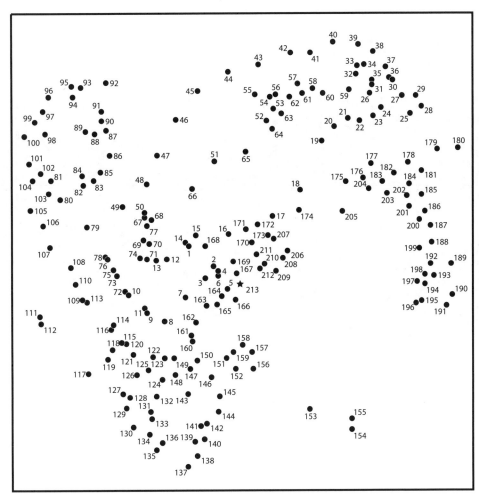

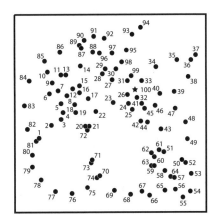

ANSWERS, PAGE 78

7

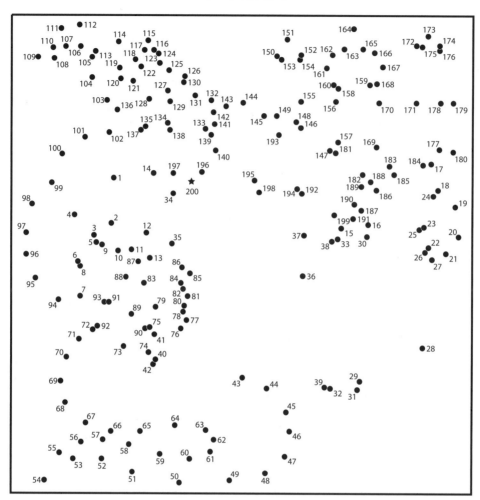

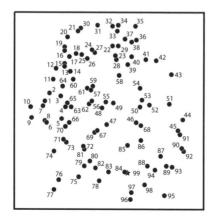

ANSWERS, PAGE 78

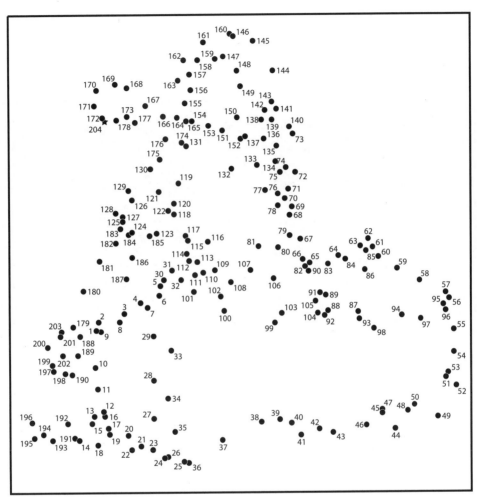

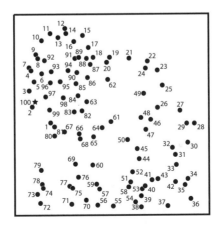

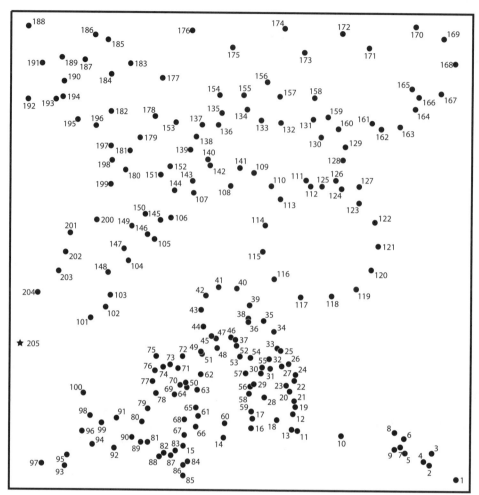

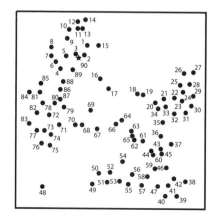

ANSWERS, PAGE 79

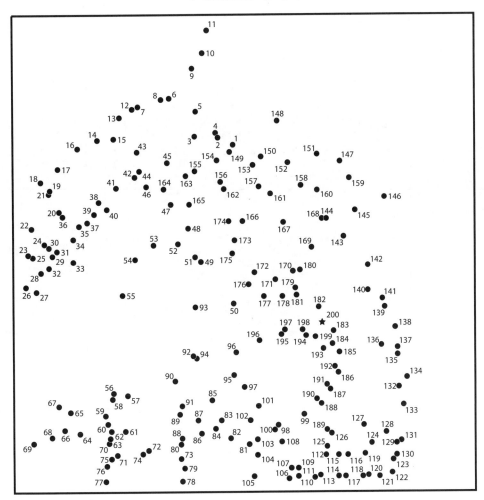

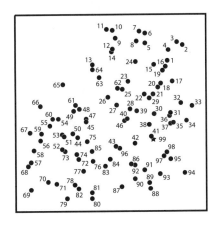

ANSWERS, PAGE 79

11

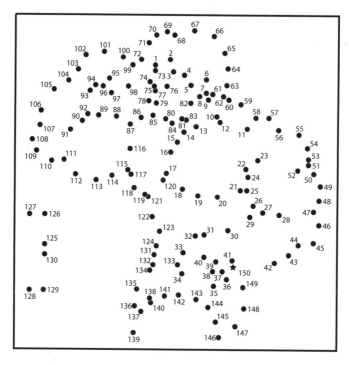

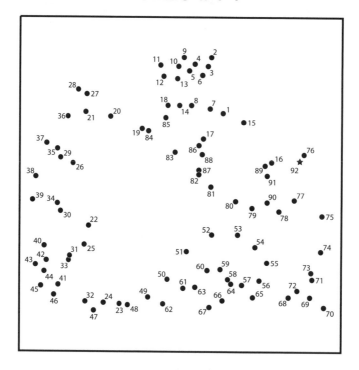

ANSWERS, PAGE 80

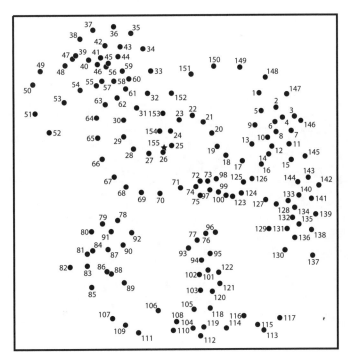

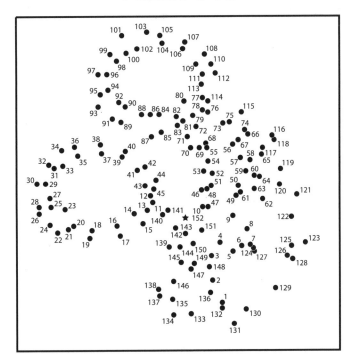

ANSWERS, PAGE 80

13

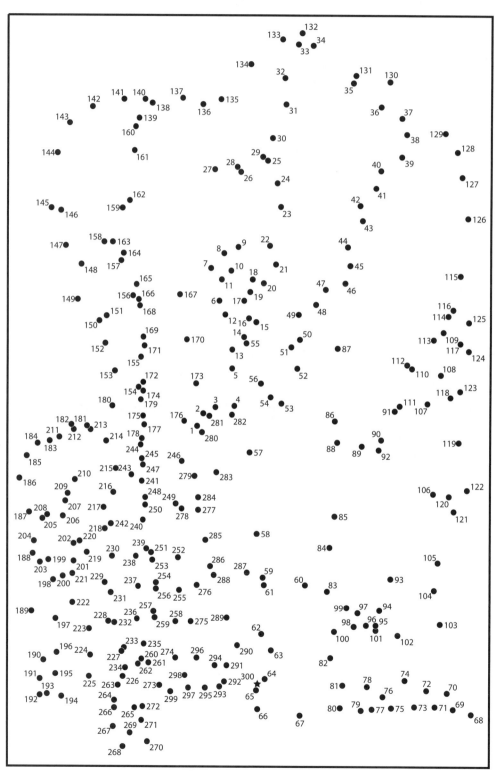

ANSWER, PAGE 81

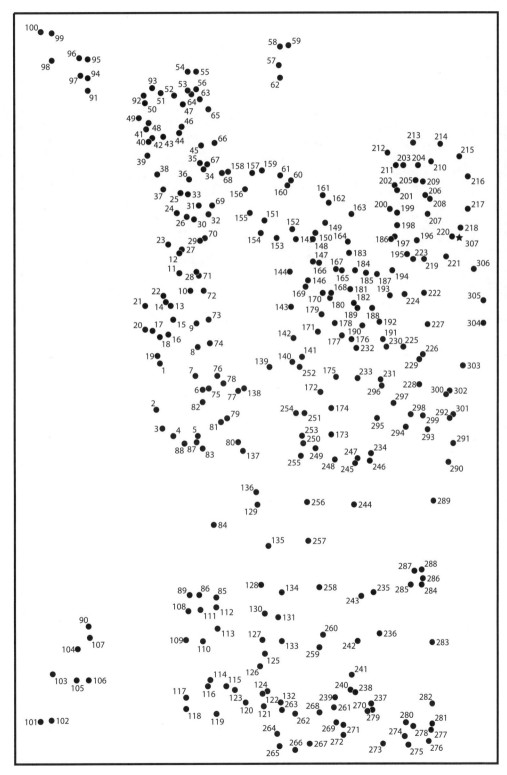

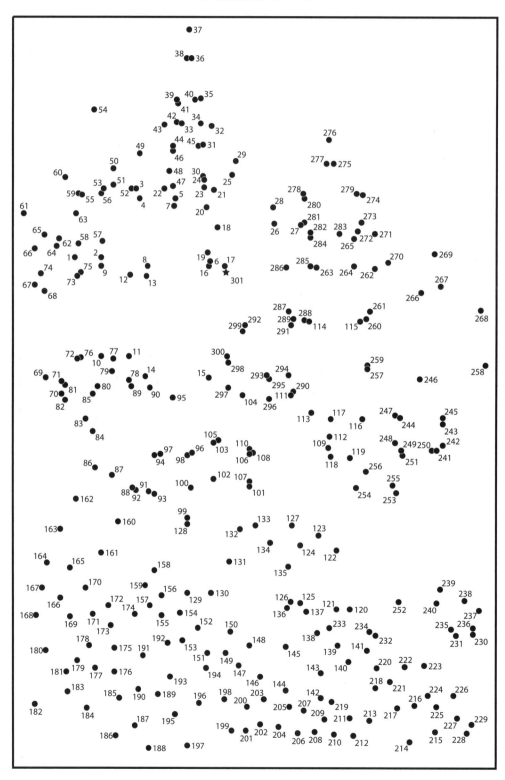

ANSWER, PAGE 81

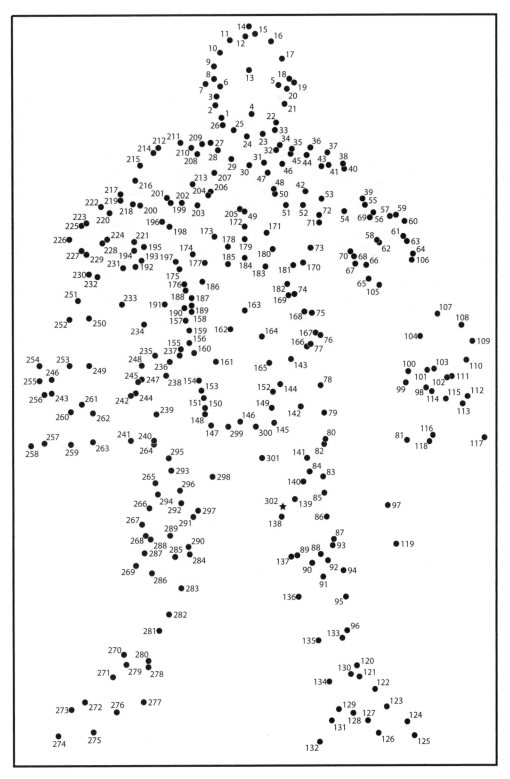

ANSWER, PAGE 81

17

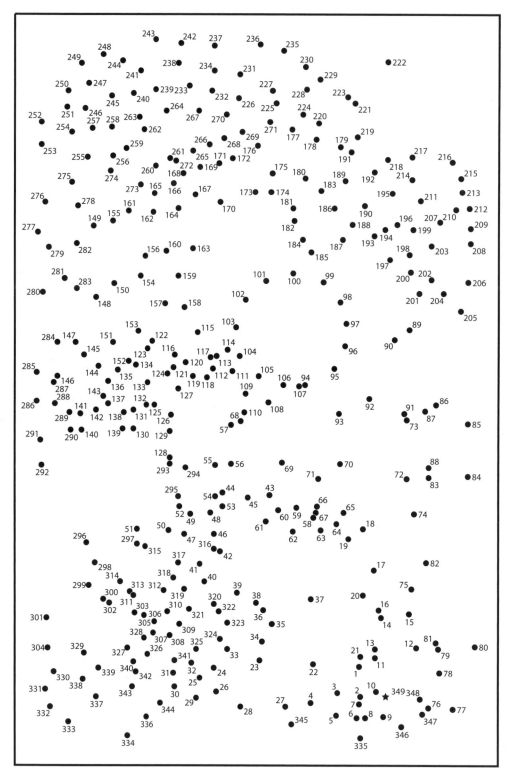

ANSWER, PAGE 82

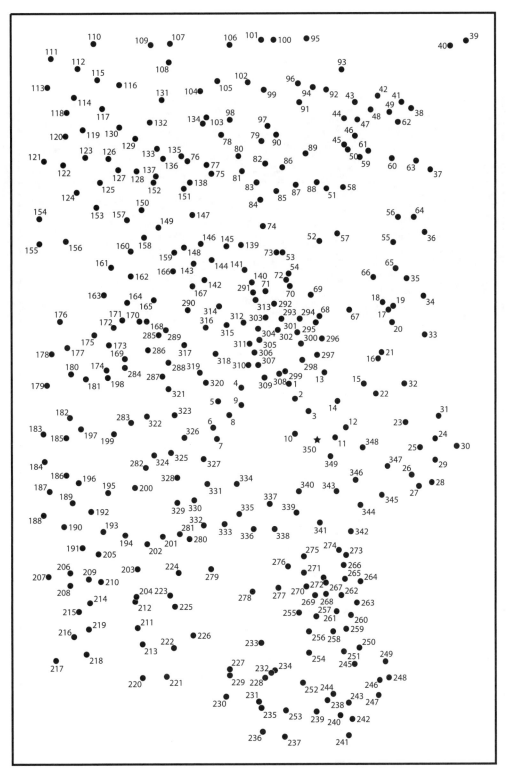

ANSWER, PAGE 82

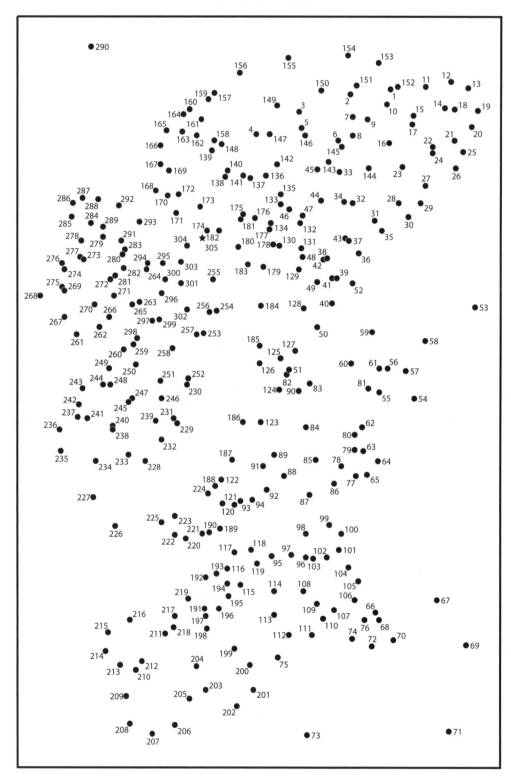

ANSWER, PAGE 82

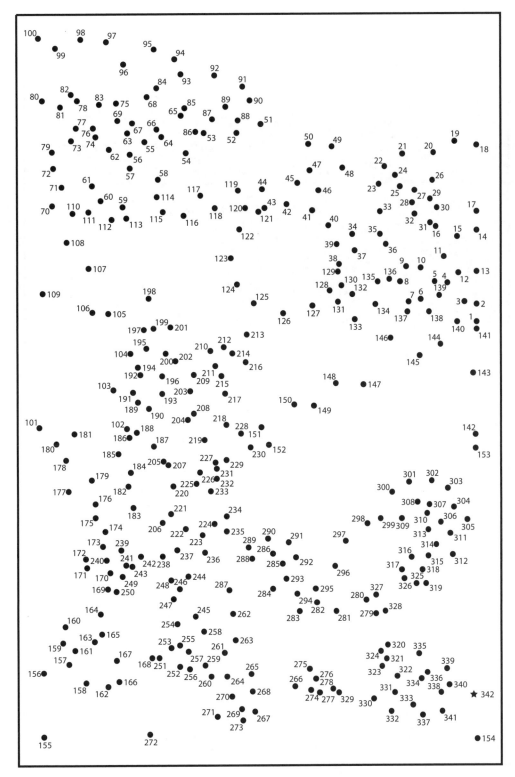

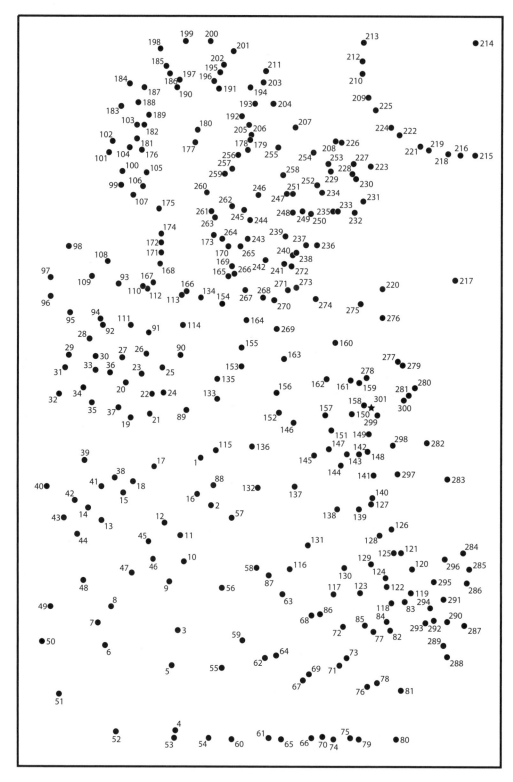

ANSWER, PAGE 83

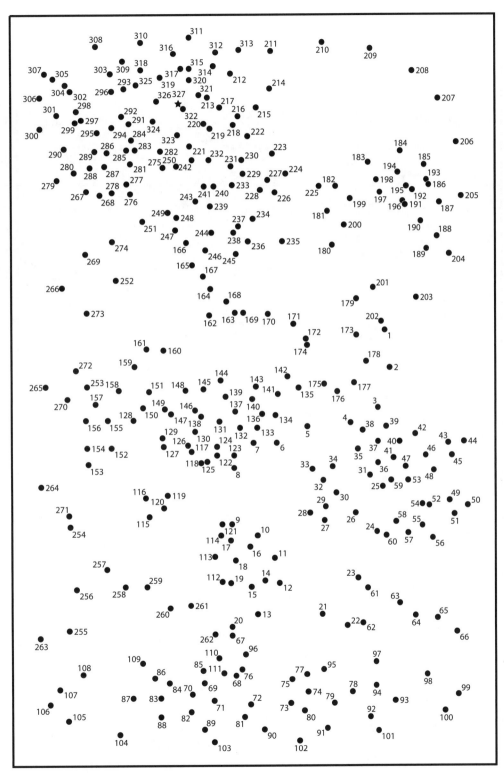

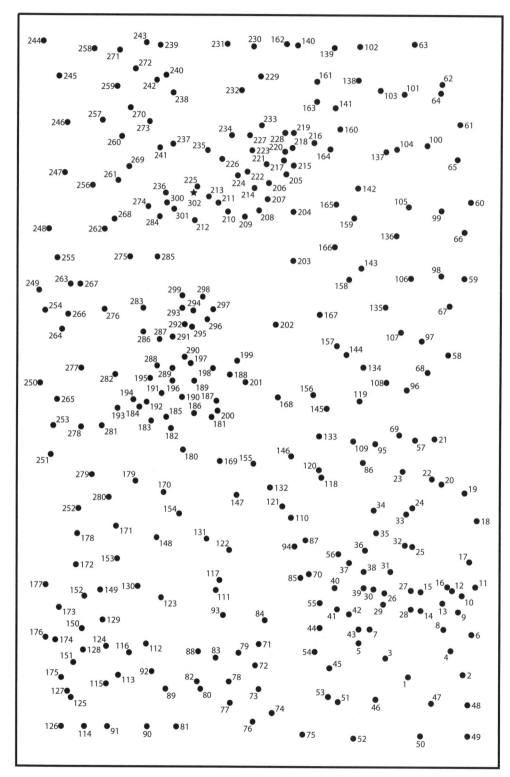

ANSWER, PAGE 83

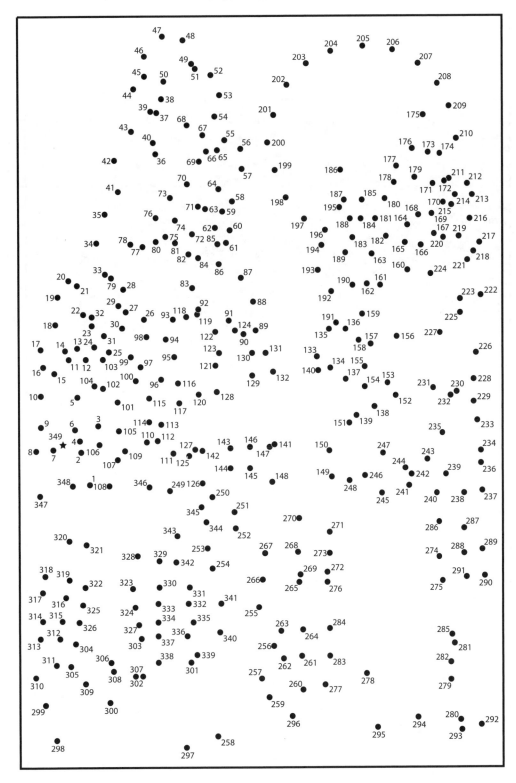

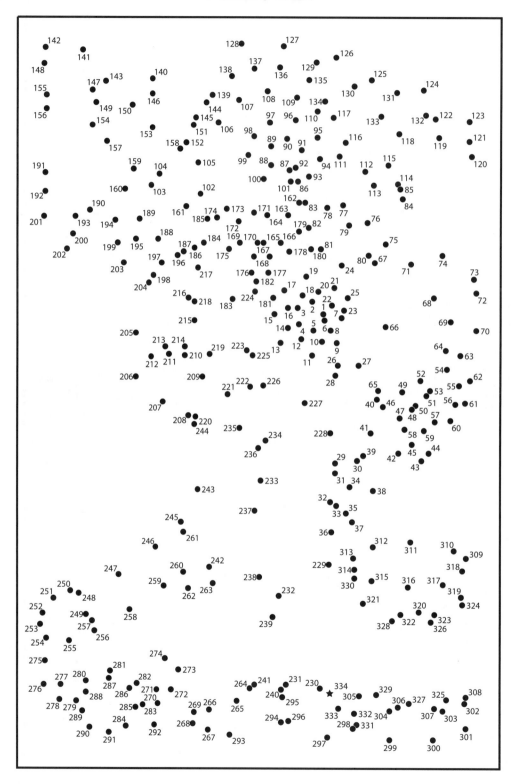

ANSWER, PAGE 84

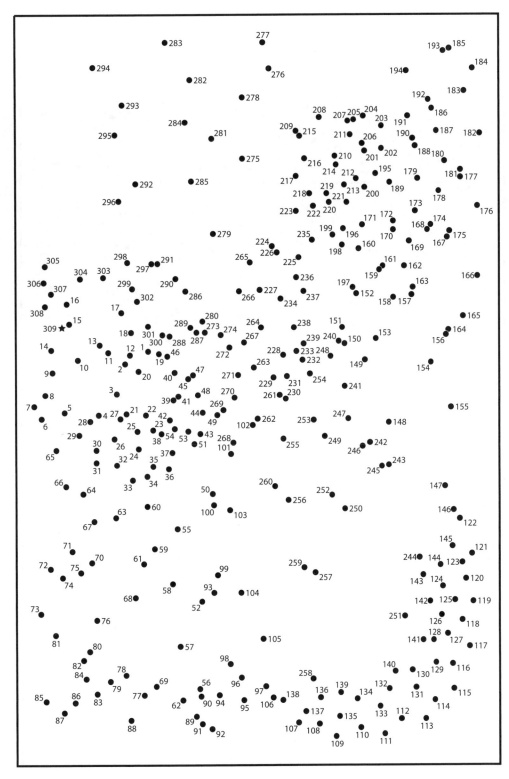

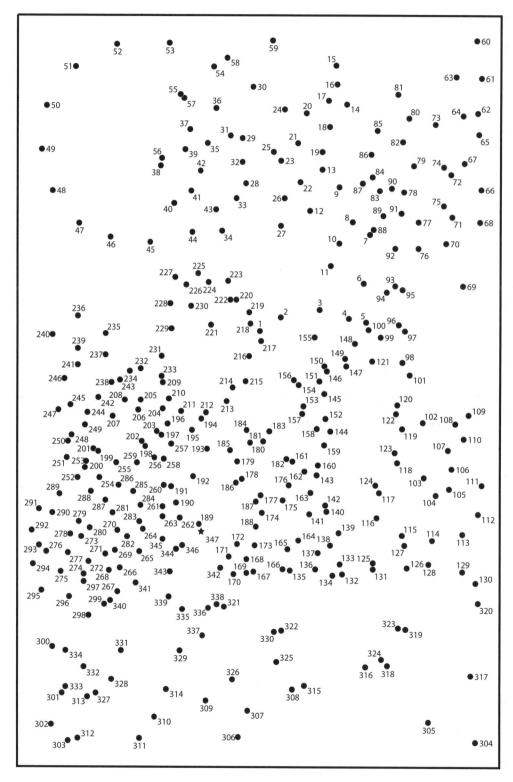

ANSWER, PAGE 84

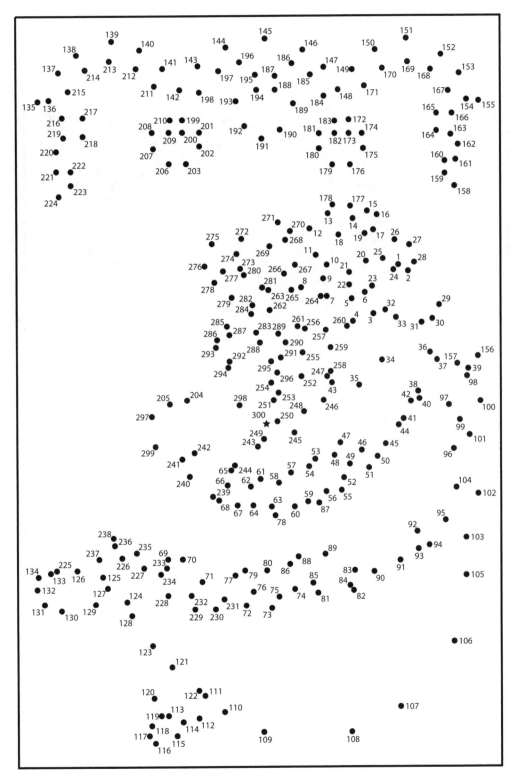

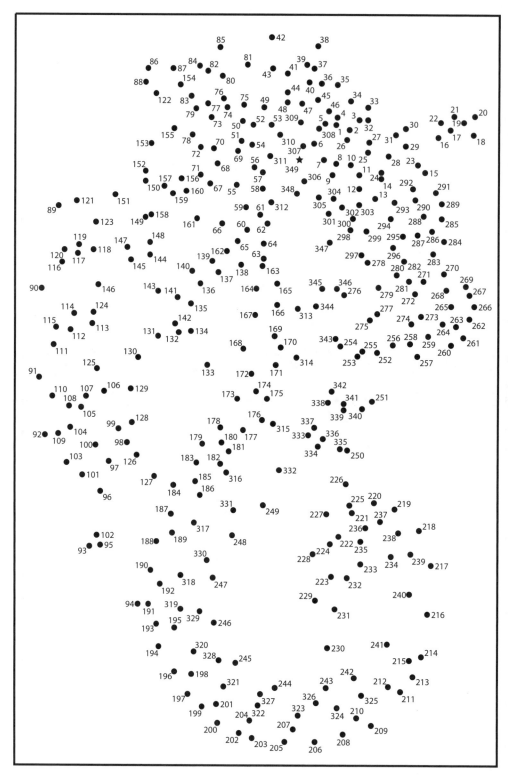

ANSWER, PAGE 85

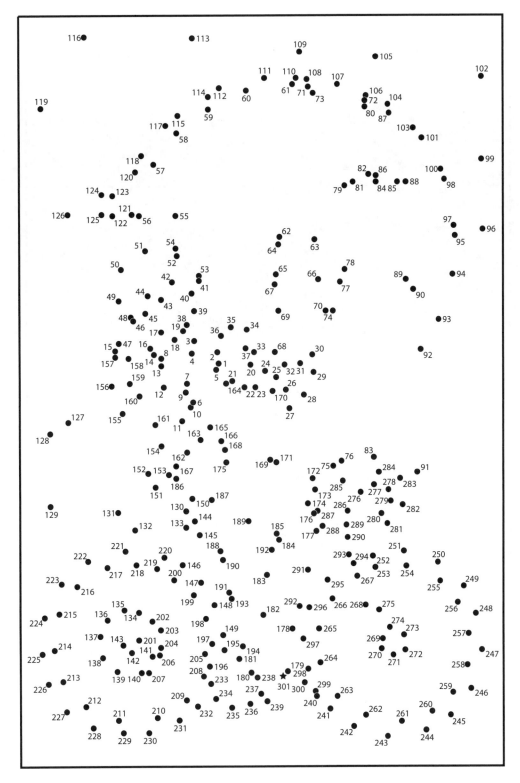

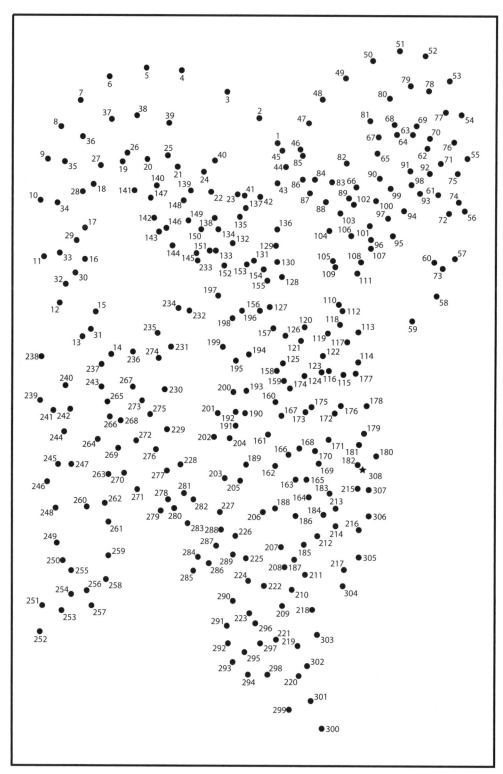

ANSWER, PAGE 85

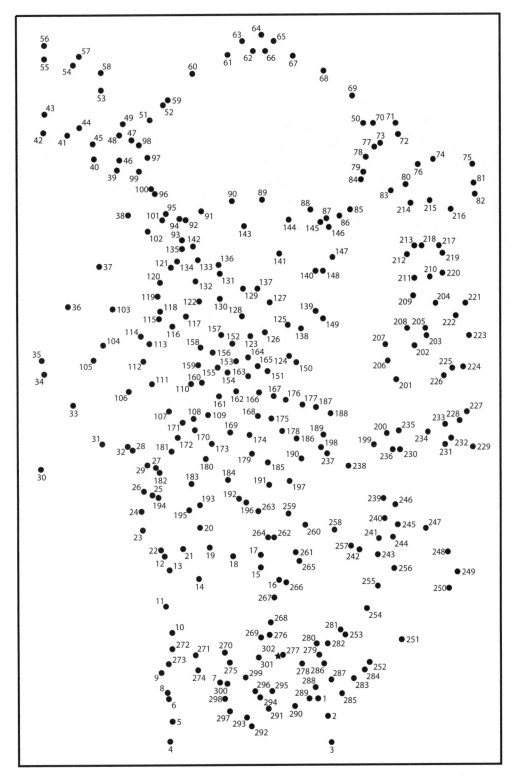

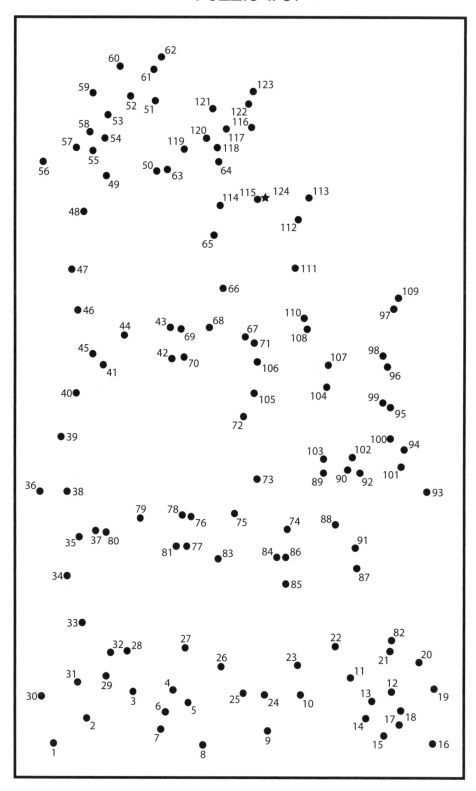

ANSWER, PAGE 86

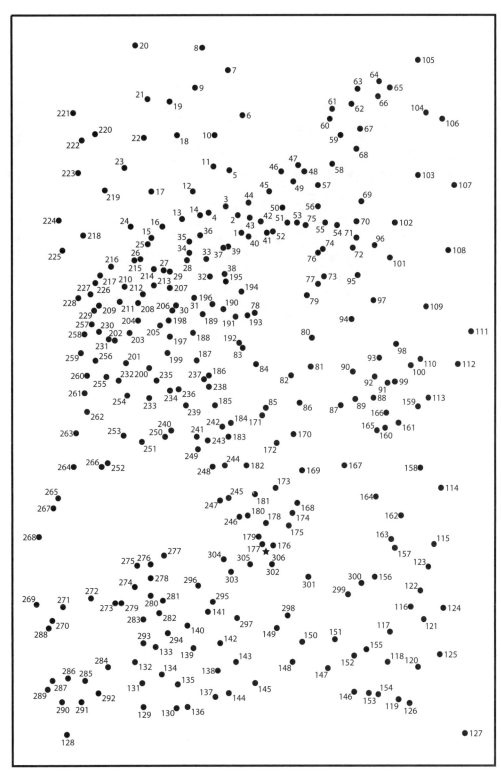

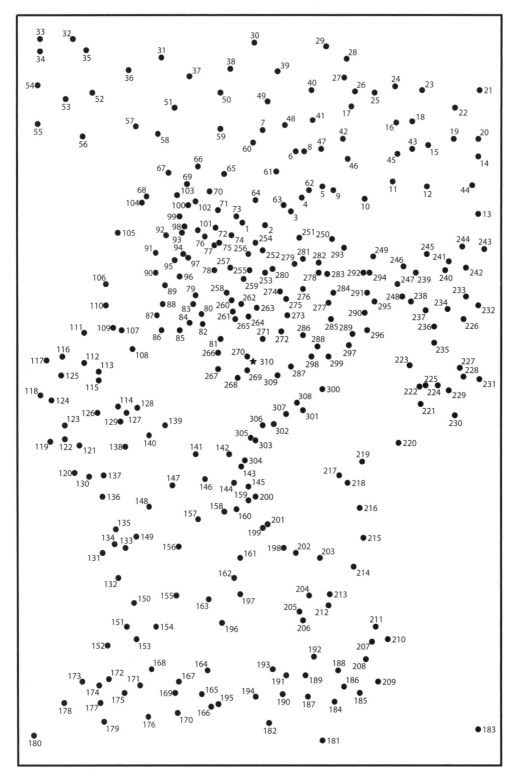

ANSWER, PAGE 86

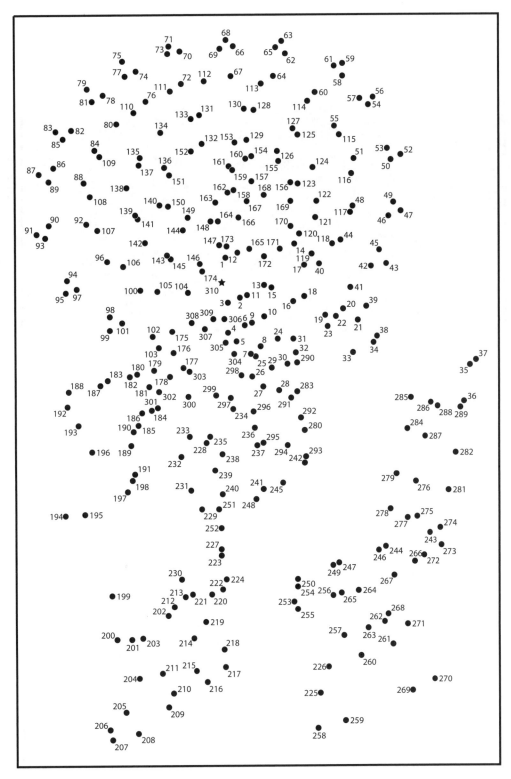

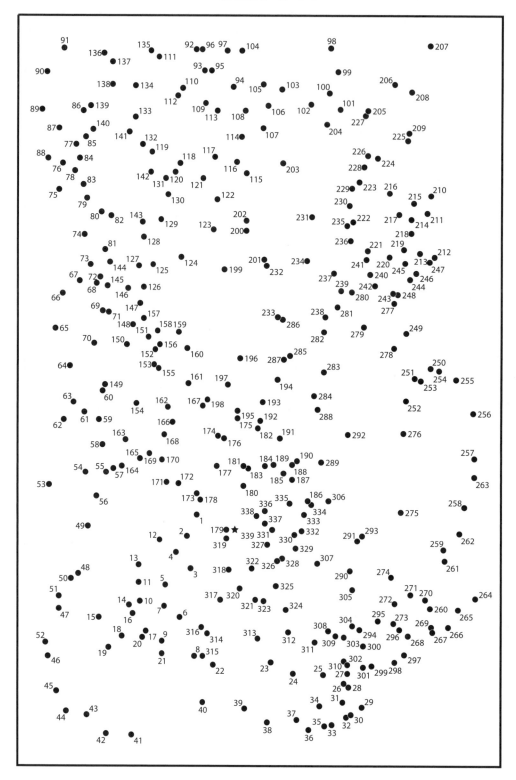

ANSWER, PAGE 87

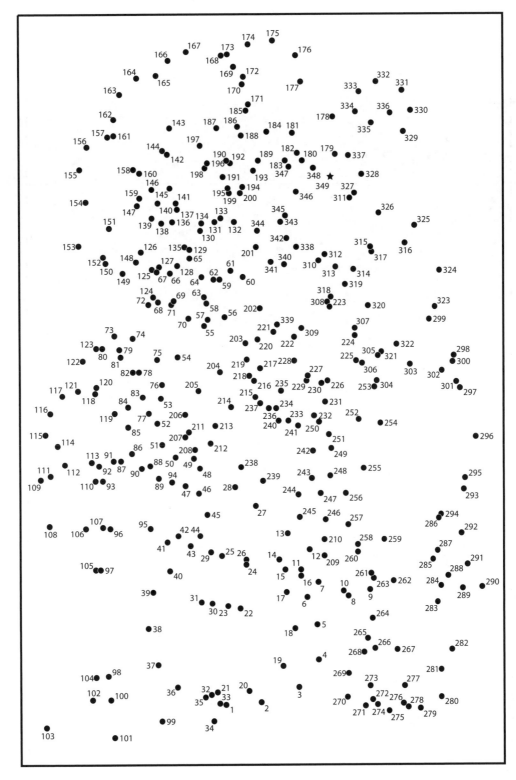

ANSWER, PAGE 87

39

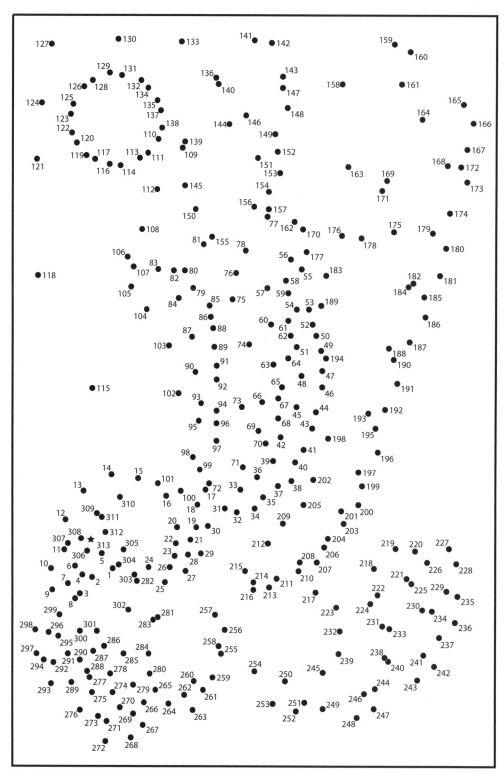

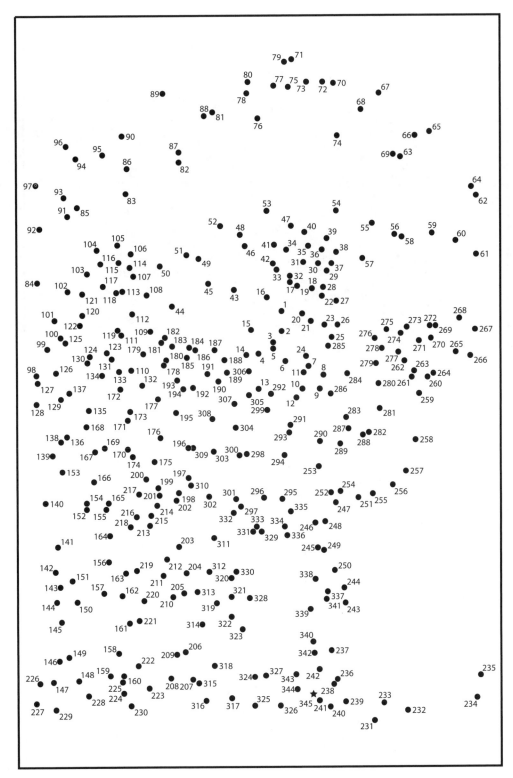

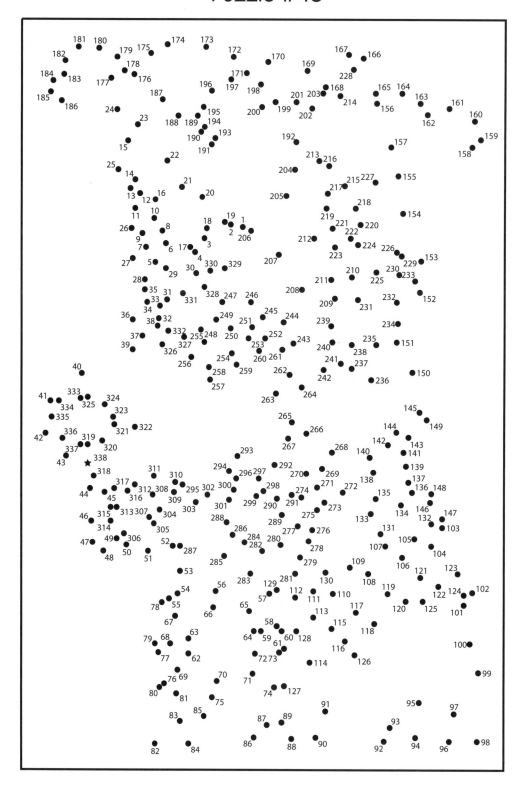

ANSWER, PAGE 88

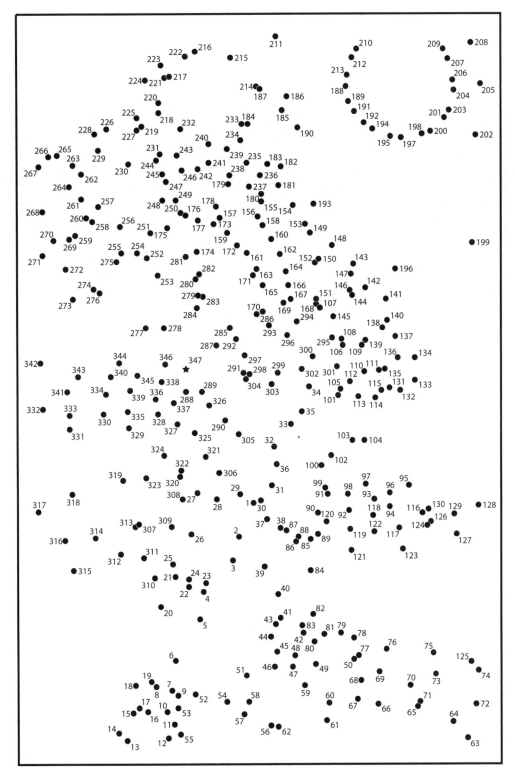

ANSWER, PAGE 88

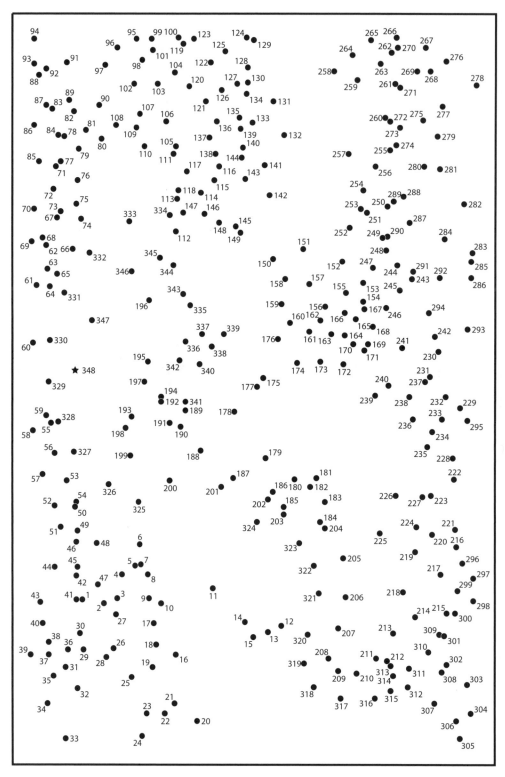

ANSWER, PAGE 88

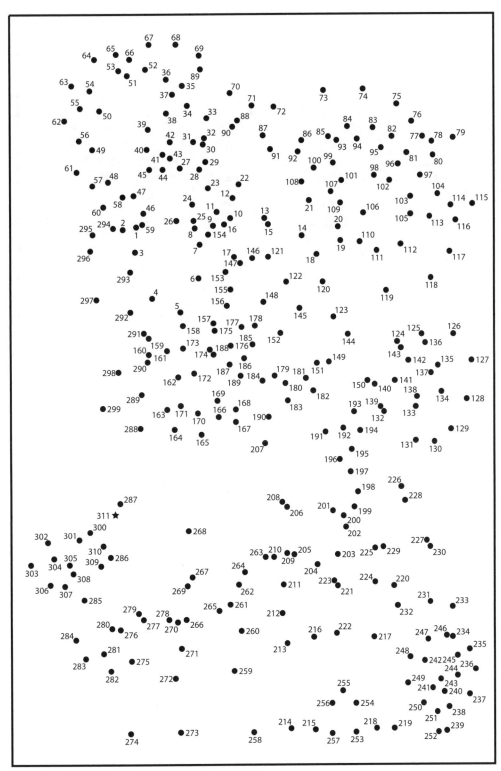

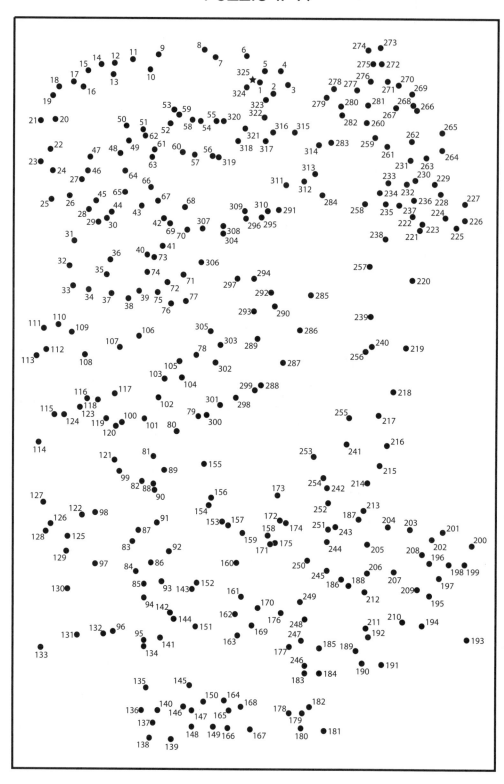

ANSWER, PAGE 89

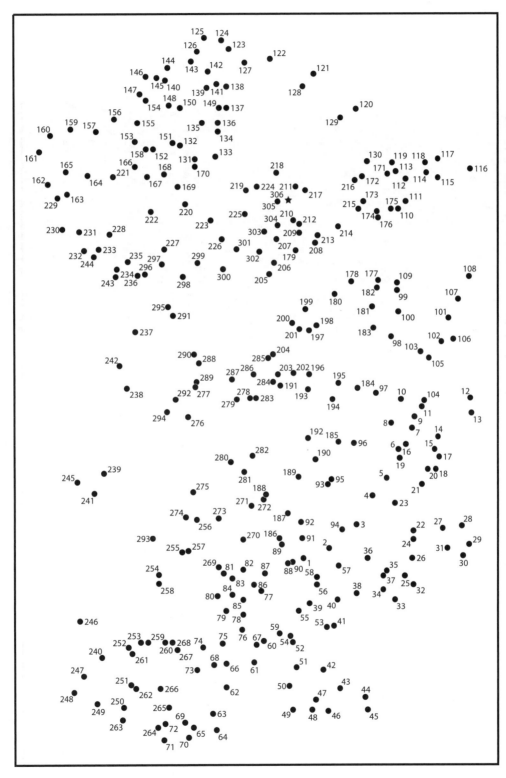

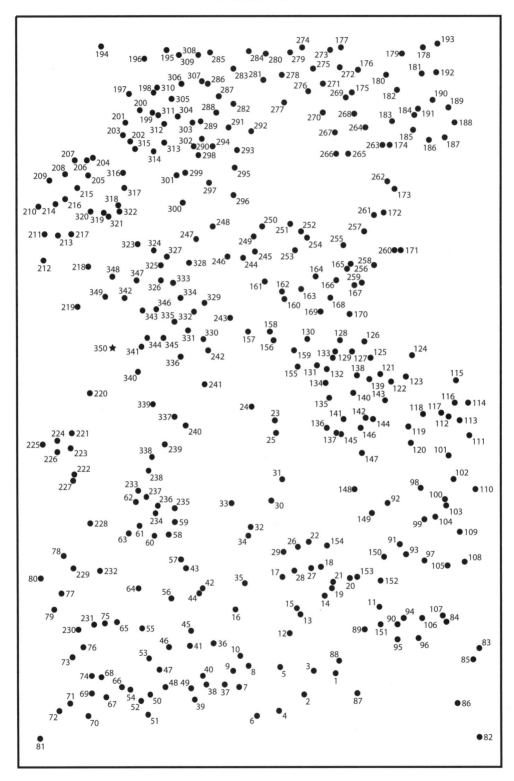

ANSWER, PAGE 89

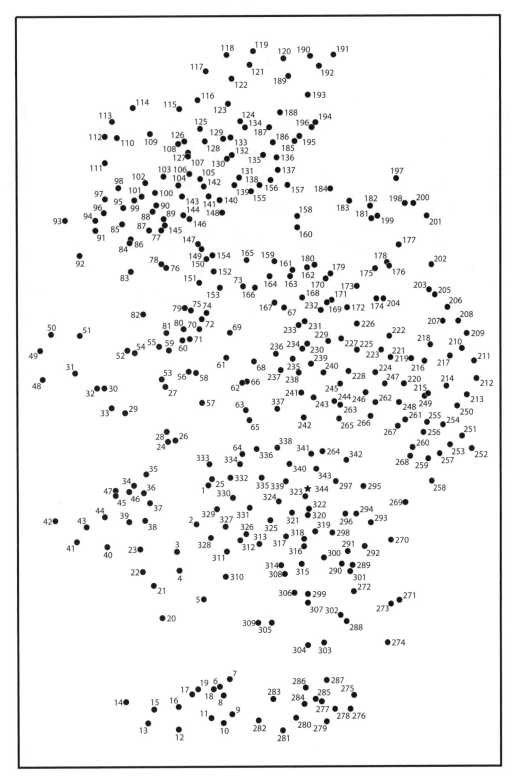

ANSWER, PAGE 89

49

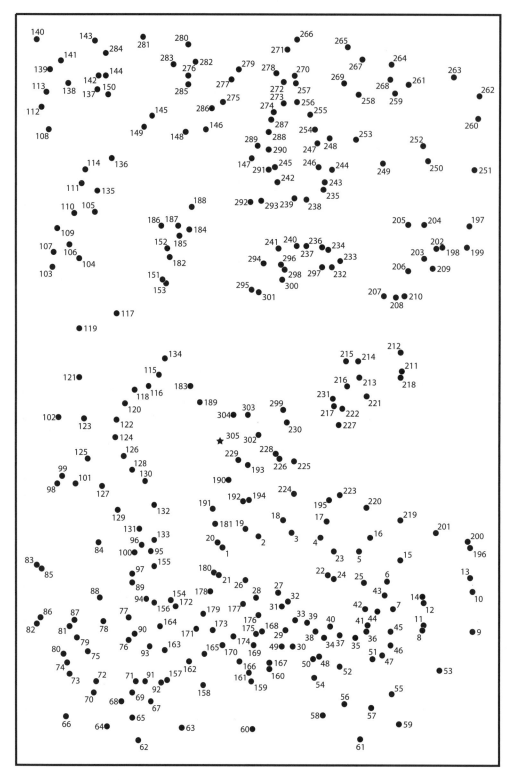

ANSWER, PAGE 90

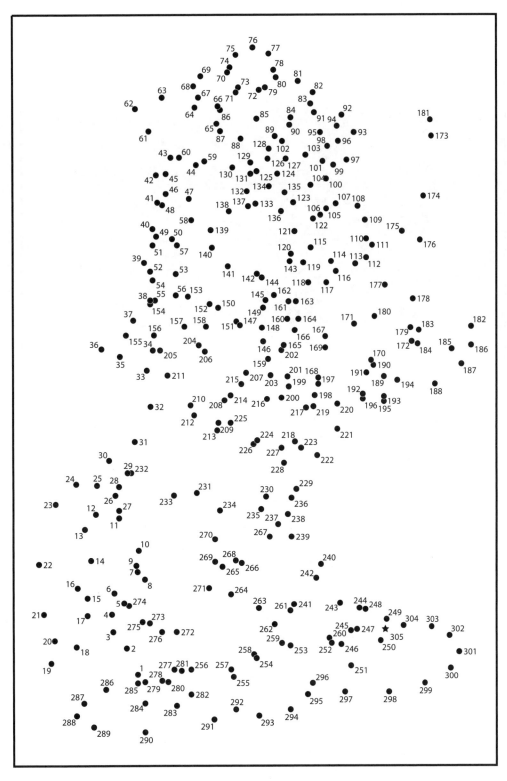

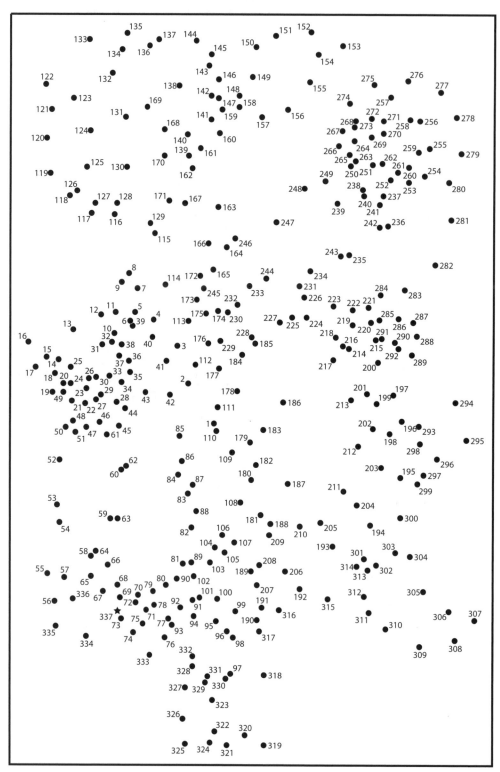

ANSWER, PAGE 90

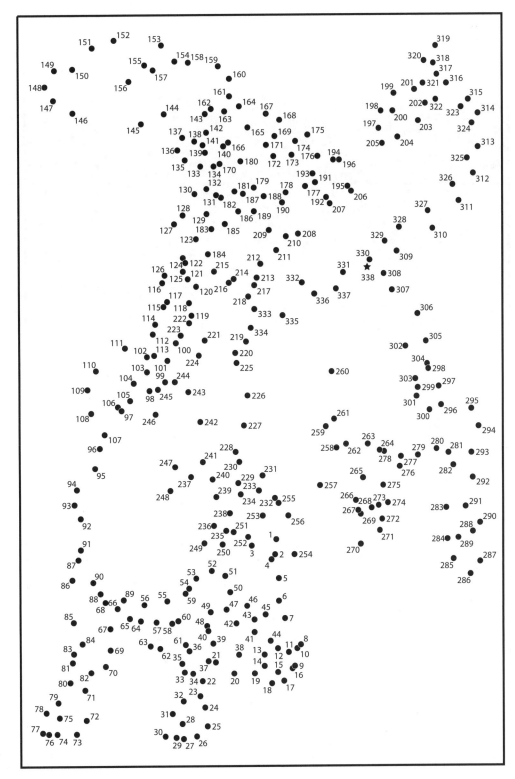

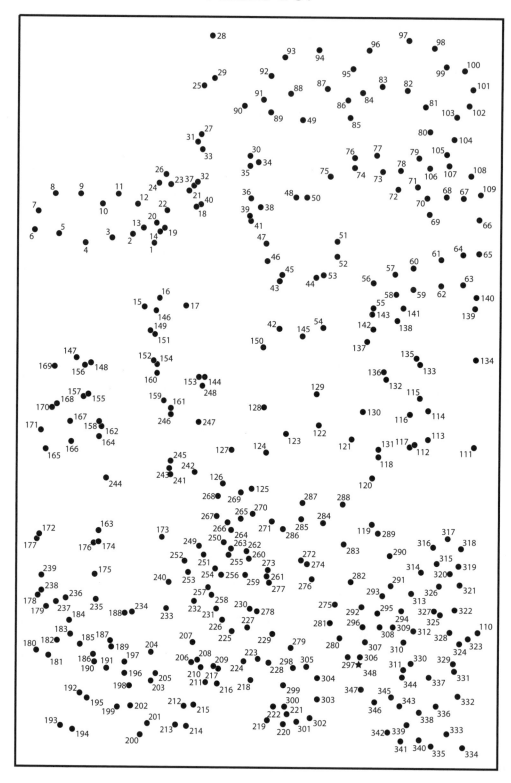

ANSWER, PAGE 91

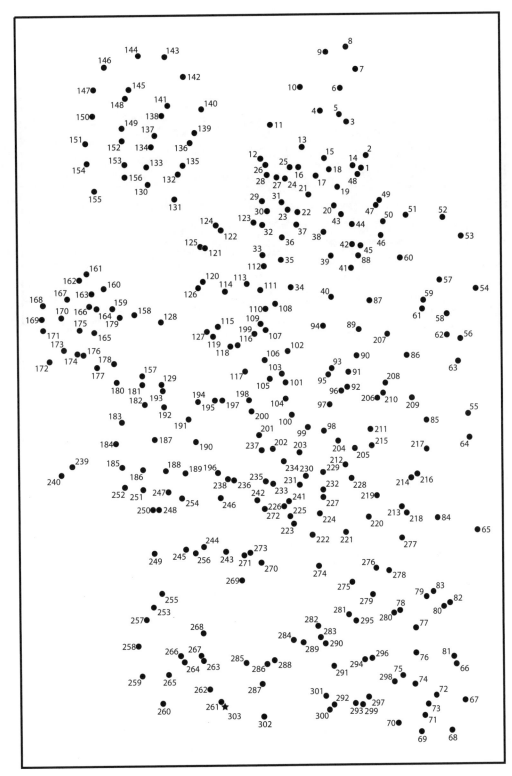

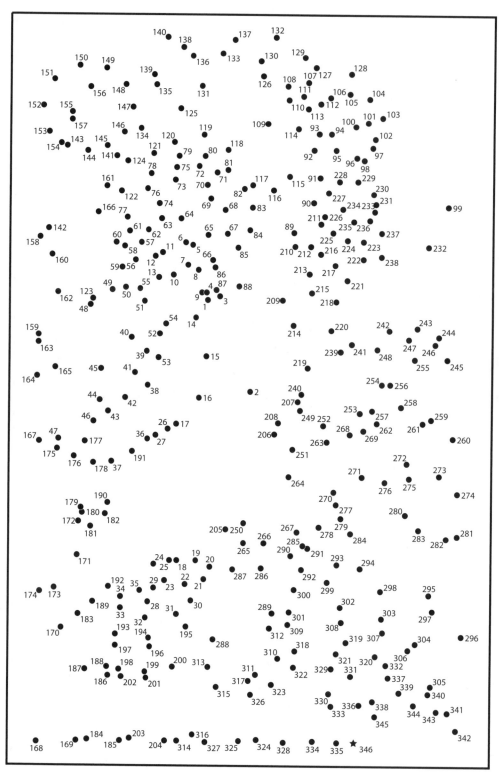

ANSWER, PAGE 91

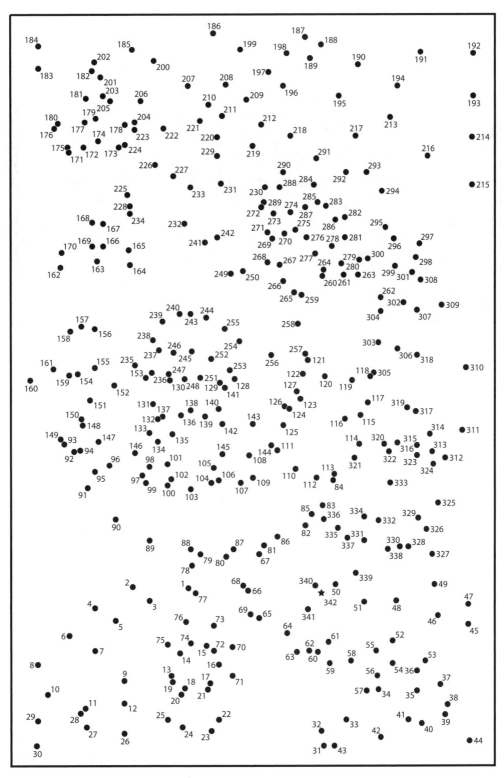

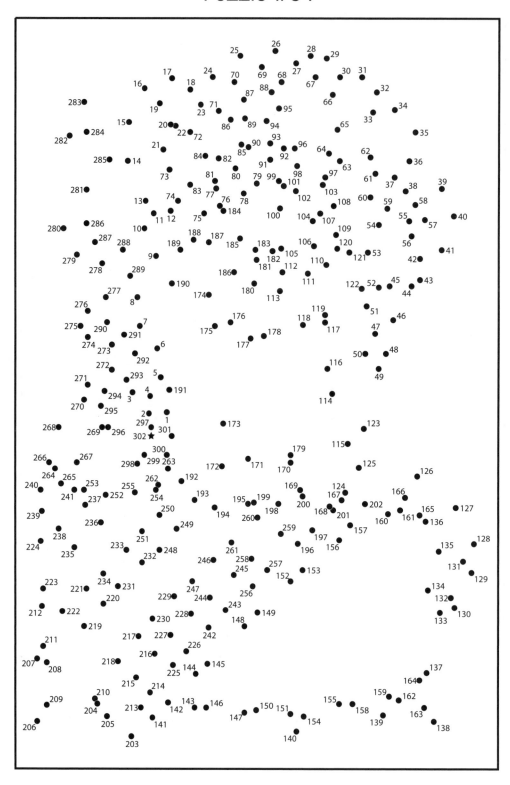

ANSWER, PAGE 92

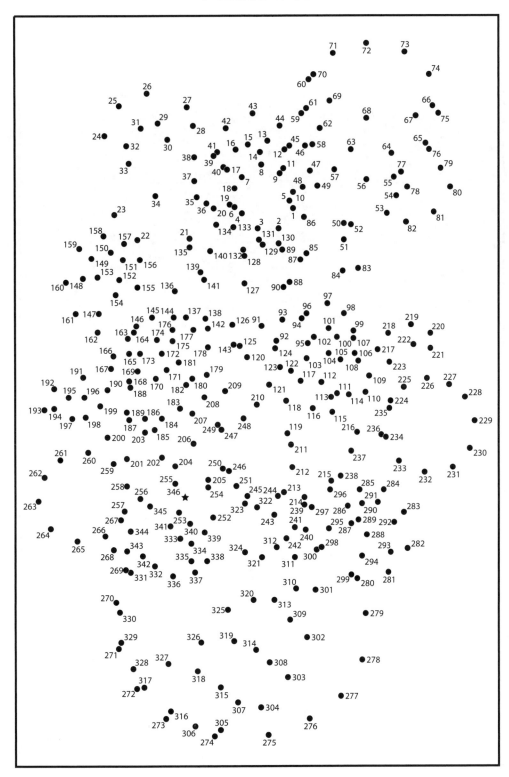

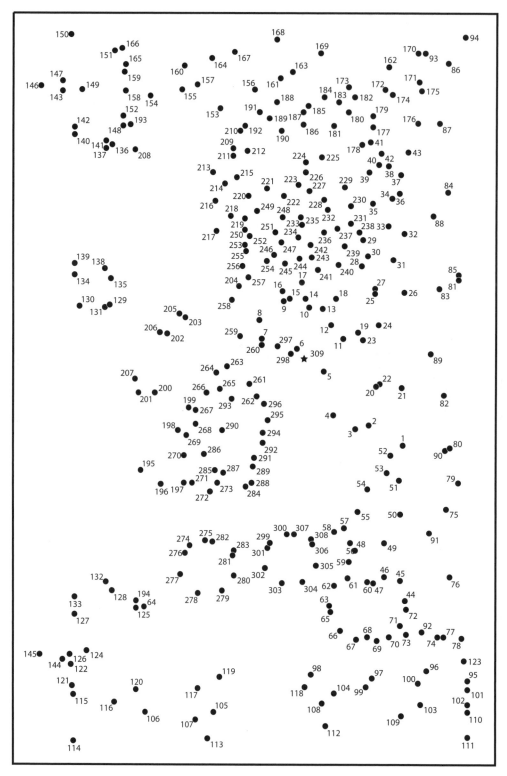

ANSWER, PAGE 92

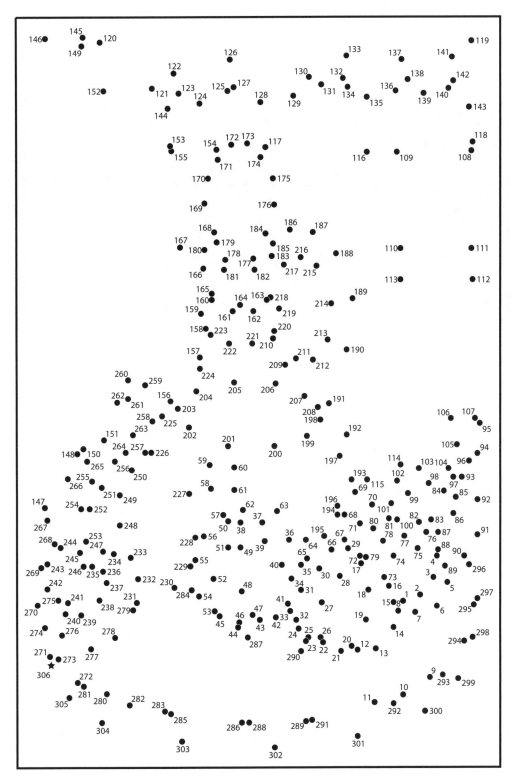

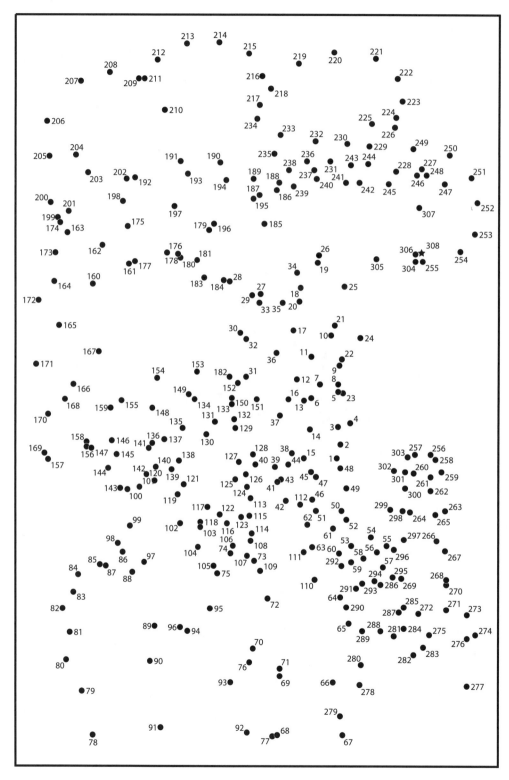

ANSWER, PAGE 93

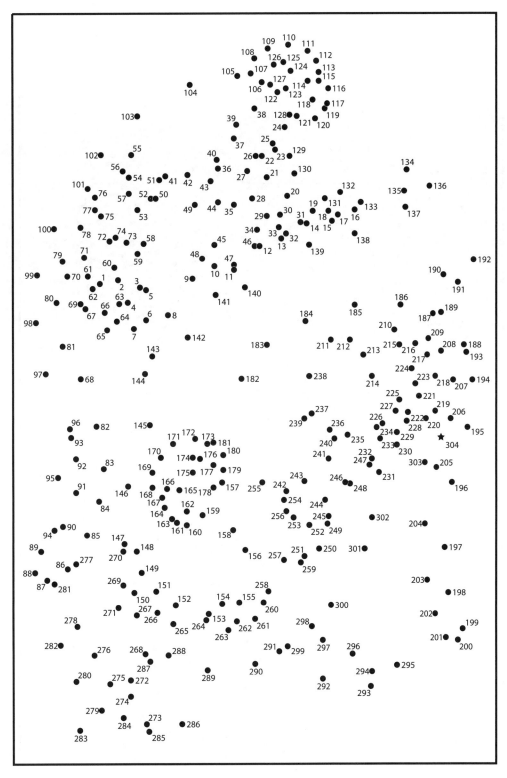

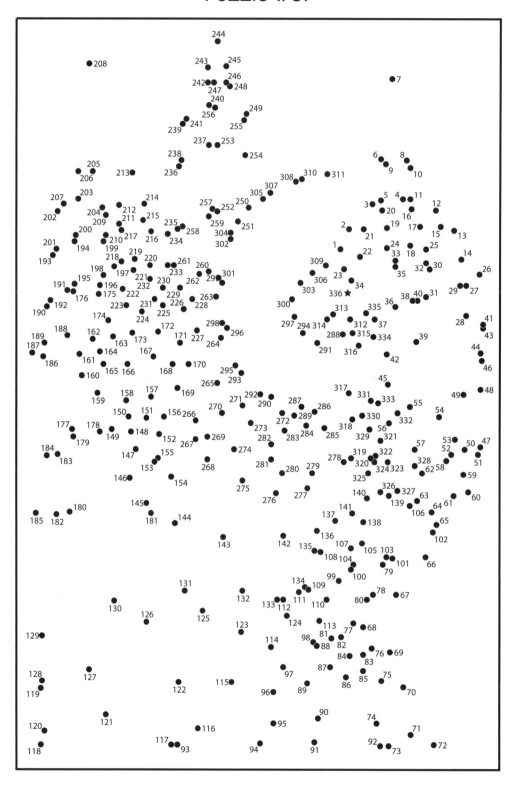

ANSWER, PAGE 93

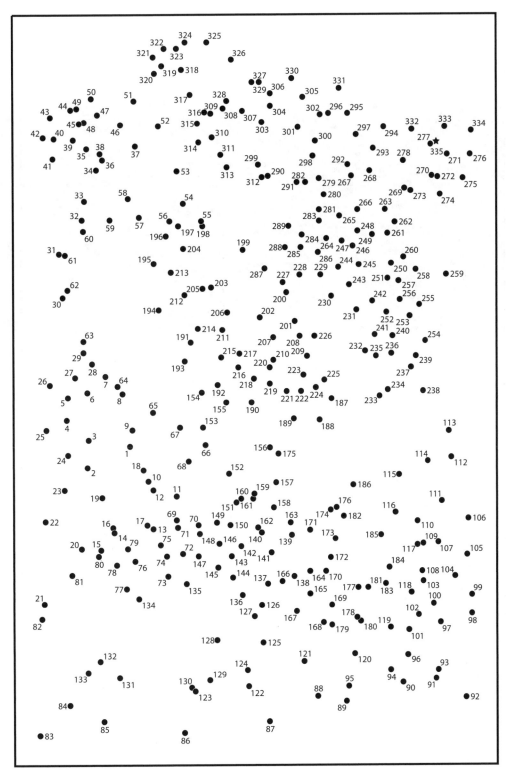

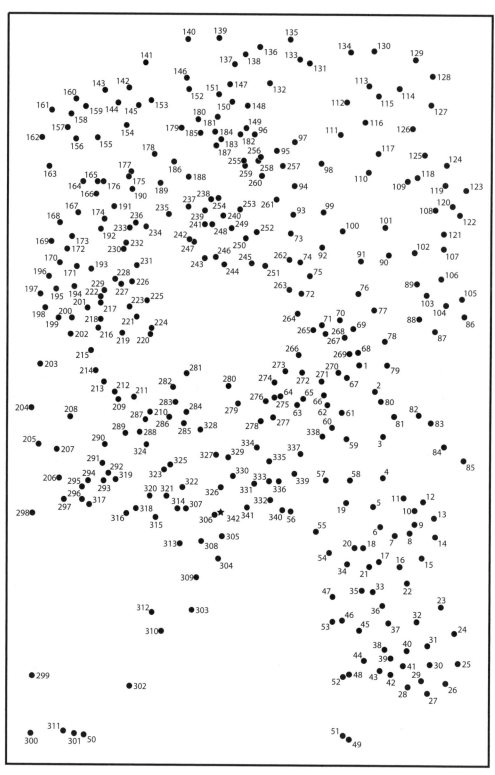

ANSWER, PAGE 94

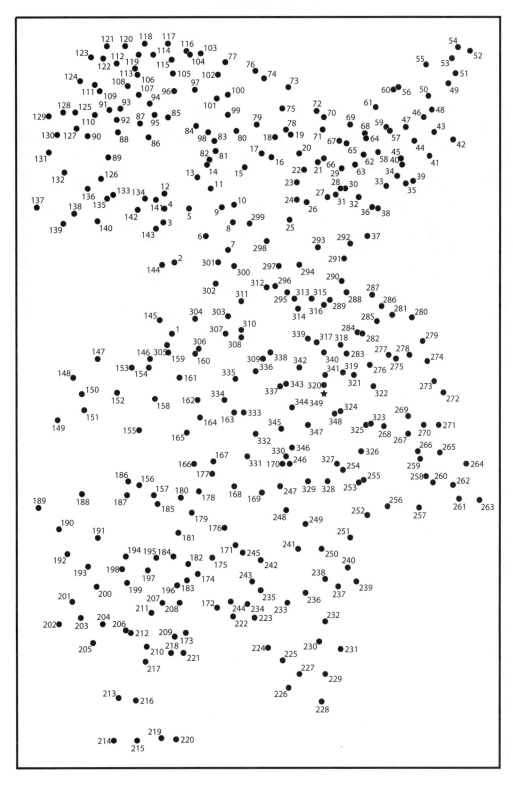

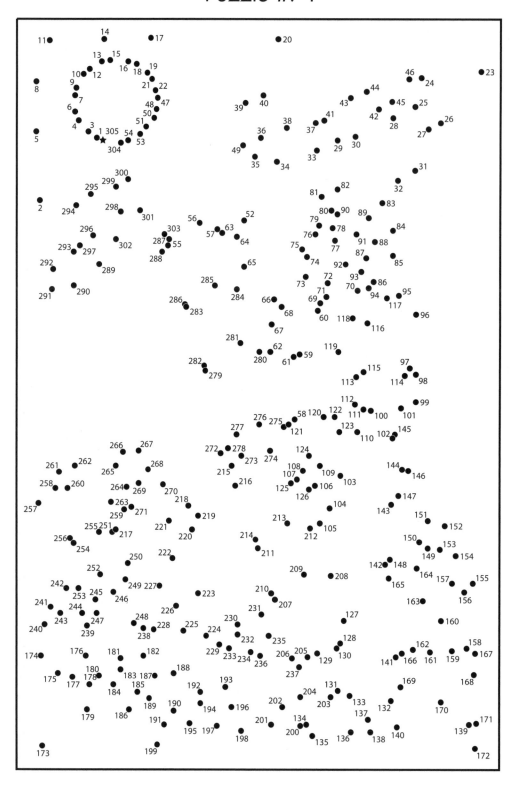

ANSWER, PAGE 94

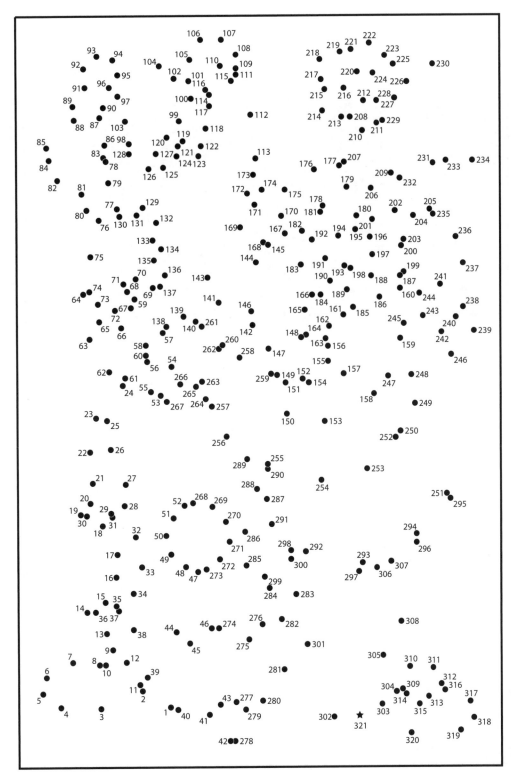

ANSWER, PAGE 94

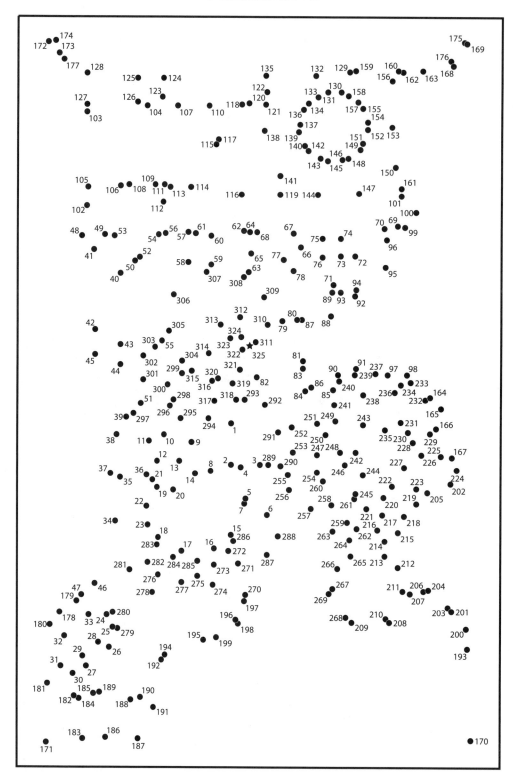

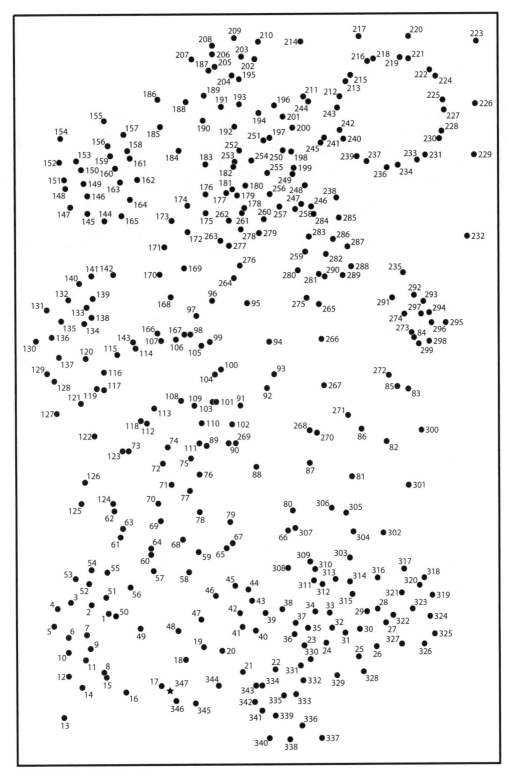

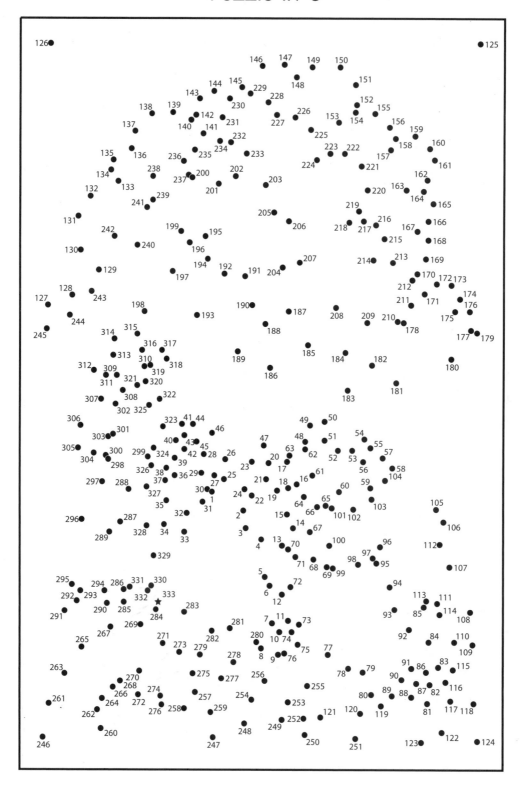

ANSWER, PAGE 95

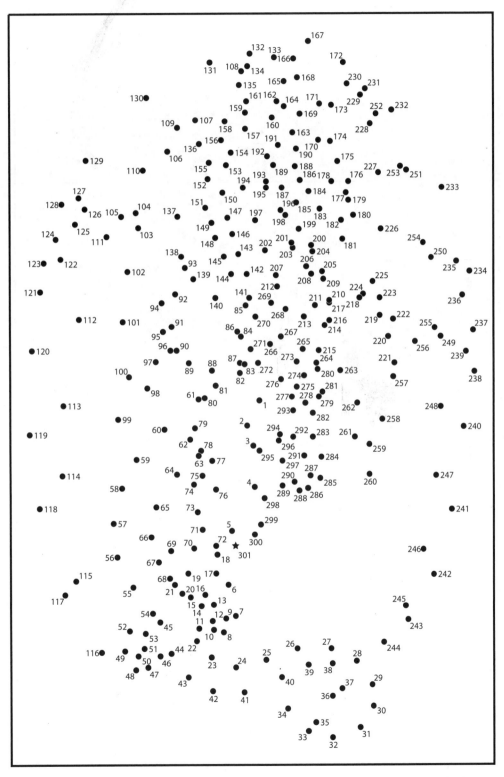

ANSWER, PAGE 95

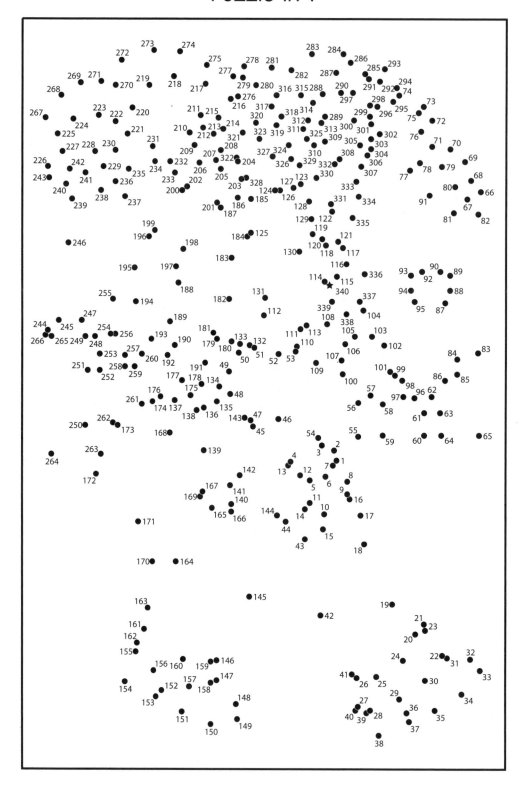

ANSWER, PAGE 96

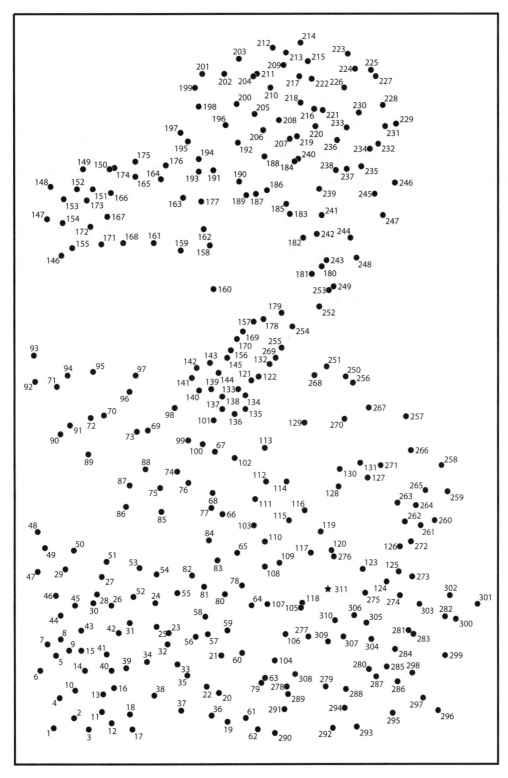

ANSWER, PAGE 96

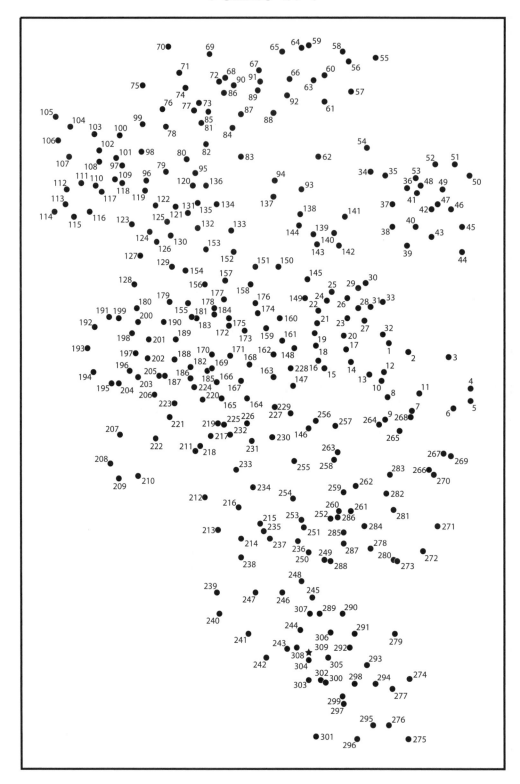

ANSWER, PAGE 96

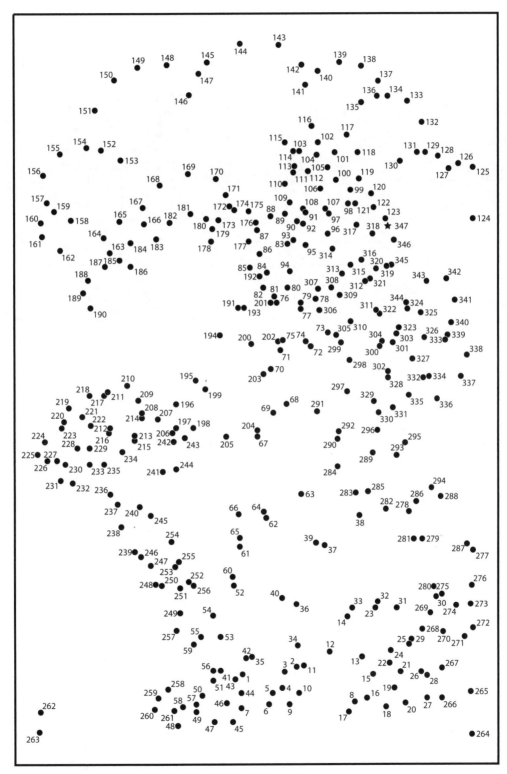

Puzzle #1

Puzzle #2

Puzzle #3

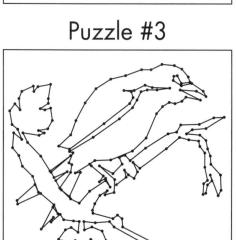

Puzzle #4

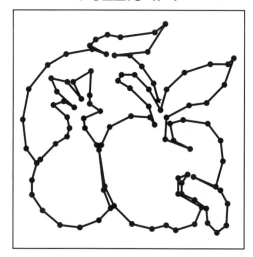

Puzzle #5

Puzzle #6

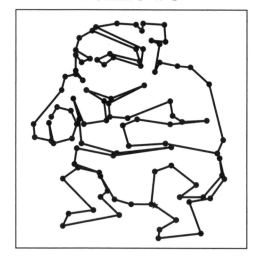

Puzzle #7

Puzzle #8

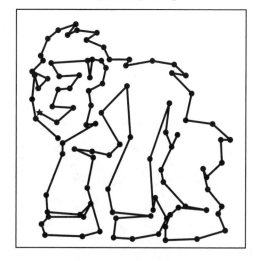

Puzzle #9

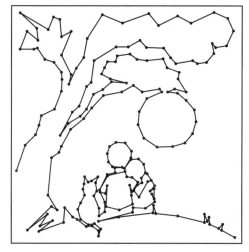

Puzzle #10

Puzzle #11

Puzzle #12

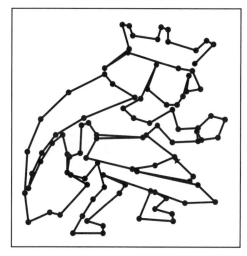

Puzzle #13

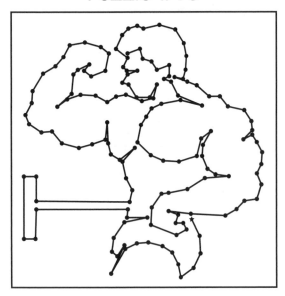

Puzzle #14

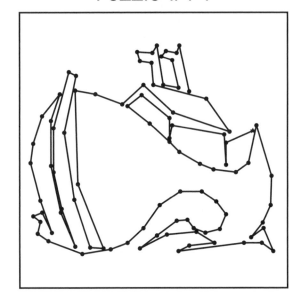

Puzzle #15

Puzzle #16

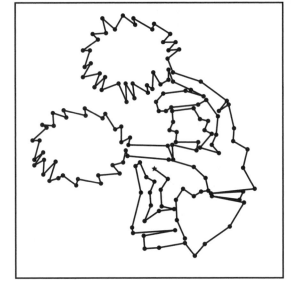

Puzzle #17

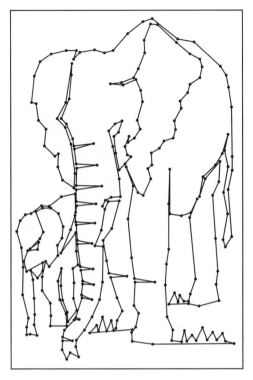

Puzzle #18

Puzzle #19

Puzzle #20

Puzzle #21

Puzzle #22

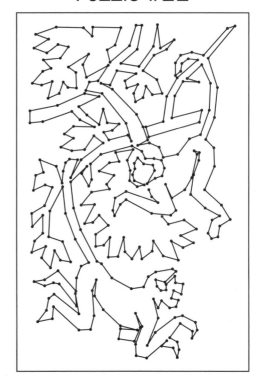

Puzzle #23

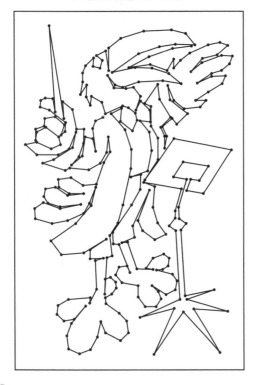

Puzzle #24

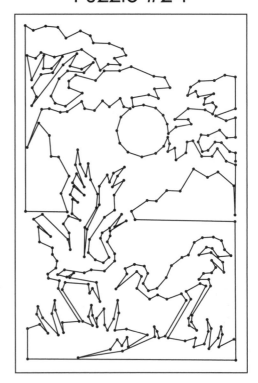

Puzzle #25

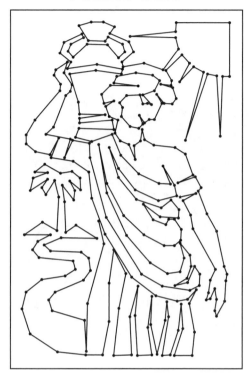

Puzzle #26

Puzzle #27

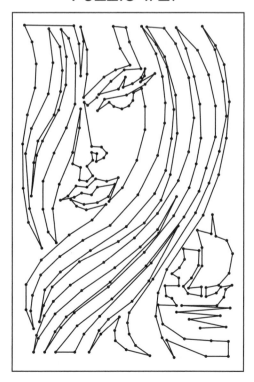

Puzzle #28

Puzzle #29

Puzzle #30

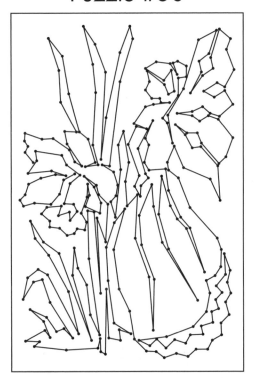

Puzzle #31

Puzzle #32

Puzzle #33

Puzzle #34

Puzzle #35

Puzzle #36

Puzzle #37

Puzzle #38

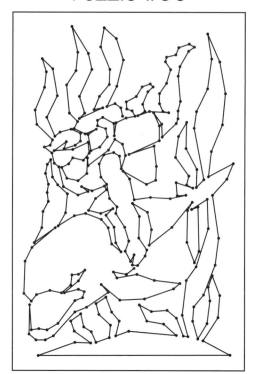

Puzzle #39

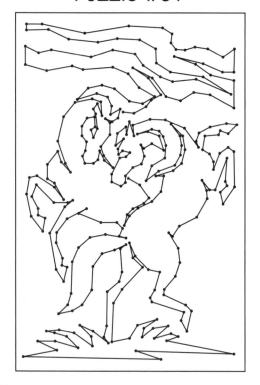

Puzzle #40

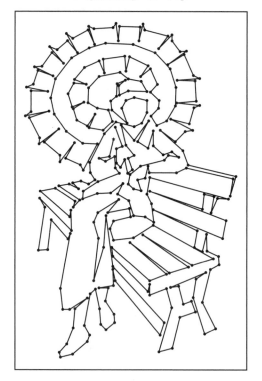

Puzzle #41

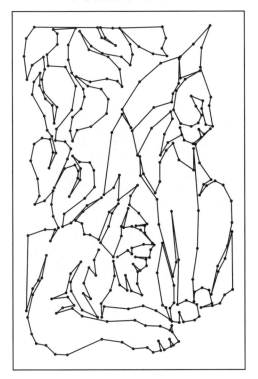

Puzzle #42

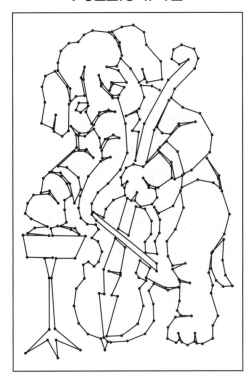

Puzzle #43

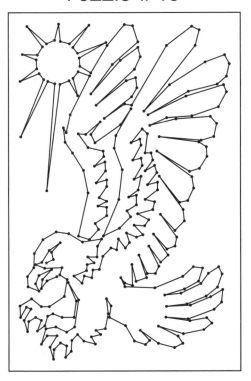

Puzzle #44

Puzzle #45

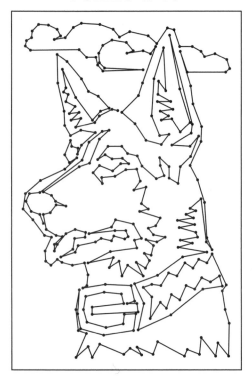

Puzzle #46

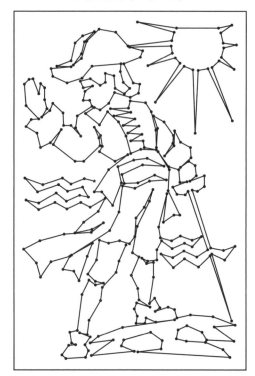

Puzzle #47

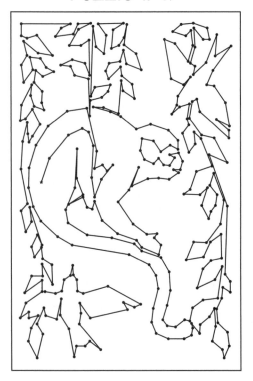

Puzzle #48

Puzzle #49

Puzzle #50

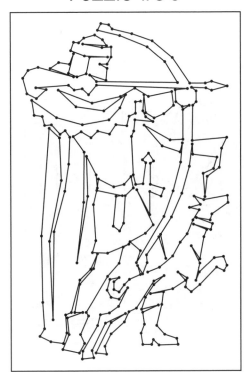

Puzzle #51

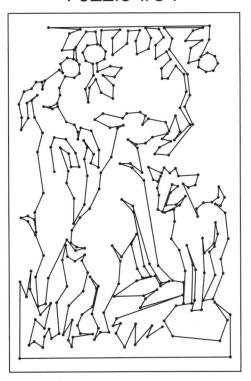

Puzzle #52

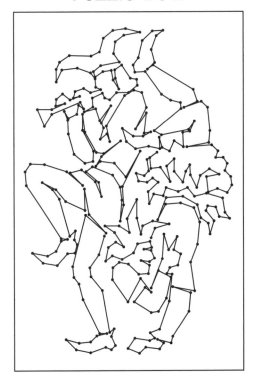

Puzzle #53

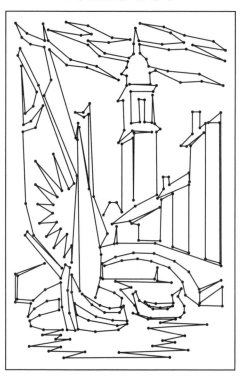

Puzzle #54

Puzzle #55

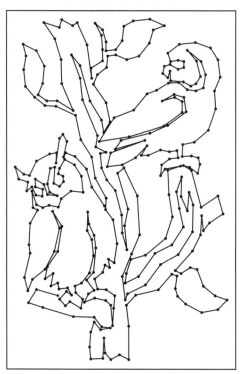

Puzzle #56

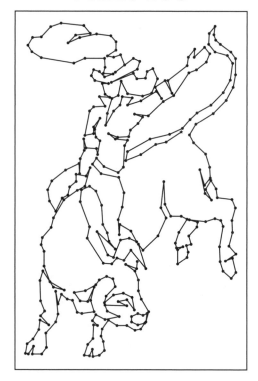

Puzzle #57

Puzzle #58

Puzzle #59

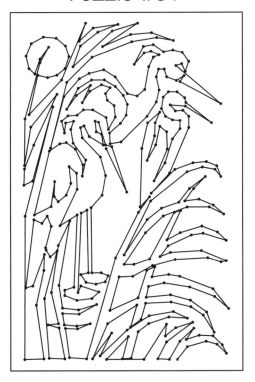

Puzzle #60

Puzzle #61

Puzzle #62

Puzzle #63

Puzzle #64

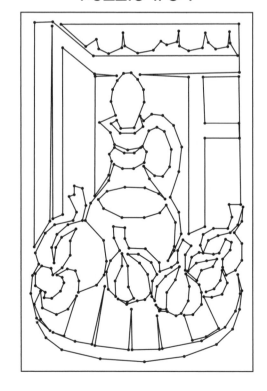

Puzzle #65

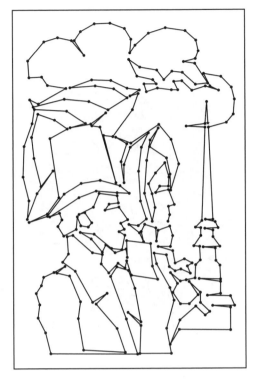

Puzzle #66

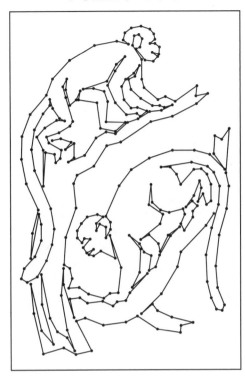

Puzzle #67

Puzzle #68

Puzzle #69

Puzzle #70

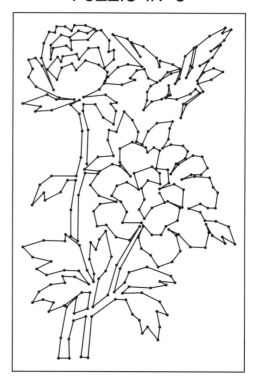

Puzzle #71

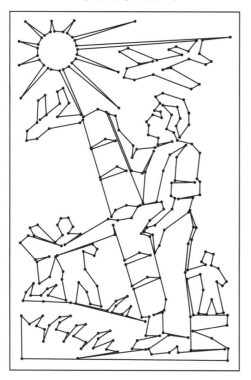

Puzzle #72

Puzzle #73

Puzzle #74

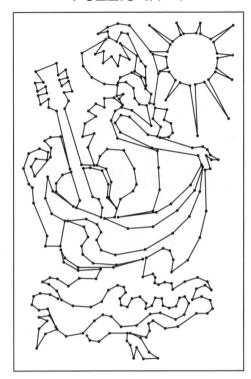

Puzzle #75

Puzzle #76

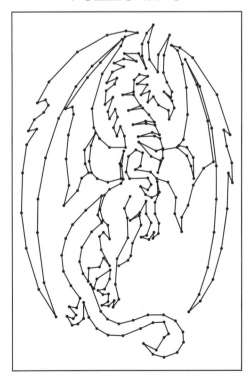

Puzzle #77

Puzzle #78

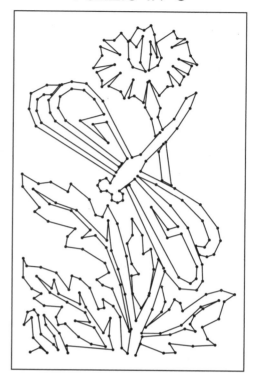

Puzzle #79

Puzzle #80